T0354019

Pupil's Book

2

Hopscotch

JENNIFER HEATH

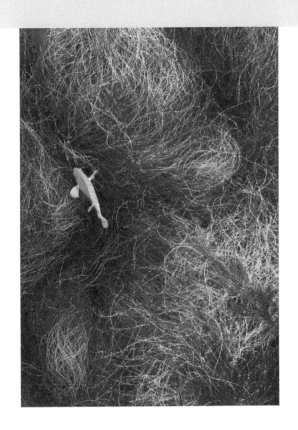

NATIONAL
GEOGRAPHIC
L E A R N I N G

Australia • Brazil • Japan • Korea • Mexico • Singapore • Spain • United Kingdom • United States

Icons and Rubrics

Icon	English	My language
	Listen	
	Say/Talk/Read	
	Sing/Chant	
	Play	
	Point	
	Stick	
	Look/Watch	
	Colour	
	Make	
	Tick/Match/Circle/Number	
	Draw	
	Write	

Contents

Family and friends

You will learn:
* to say where you are from and ask others
* to say how old you are and ask others
* to talk about family and friends.

1 **Listen and say.** 1/2

2 **Listen and chant.** 1/3

3 **Listen and play.** 1/4

I'm your aunt.

daughter   son   aunt   uncle   parents

1 Listen and say. 1/5

Story corner

2 Listen and read. 1/6

1
Daddy, this is my friend.

Nice to meet you.

2
What's your name?

My name's Yoko.

3
I'm your uncle.

I'm your aunt.

4
You're my friends!

1 Pupils learn and say the new words, paying special attention to their pronunciation. ⊃TB
2 Pupils listen to the dialogue, follow the story and read the sentences. ⊃TB

3 Read and match.

daughter

uncle

mummy

aunt

son

daddy

4 Write and read.

mummy	daddy
grandma	grandpa
sister	brother
aunt	uncle
daughter	son

5 Play.

3 Pupils read the words and match them with the photos.
4 Pupils trace over the words and read them aloud.
5 Pupils play *Chinese Whispers.* ➲TB

7

A happy family

boy   girl   grandparents   granddaughter   grandson

1 Listen and say. 1/7

2 Listen and read. 1/8

Look at this family. The boy is Anders and the girl is Linda. Their grandparents are Marit and Henrik.
Anders is a good grandson and Linda is a good granddaughter.
They are a happy family.

1 Pupils learn and say the new words, paying special attention to their pronunciation. ⊃TB
2 Pupils listen to the recording, follow the text and read it aloud. ⊃TB

3 Look, circle and read.

1 Linda is a   boy   girl   **.**

2 Anders is a   boy   girl   **.**

3 Marit and Henrik are   parents   grandparents **.**

4 The family is   sad   happy **.**

4 Listen and tick. 1/9

1

2

3

4

5 Play.

3 Pupils circle the correct words and read the sentences aloud.
4 Pupils listen to the recording and tick the correct picture. ⮑TB
5 Pupils play *Hunt the Thimble.* ⮑TB

9

Lesson 3

I'm from England.

Poland   America   England   Japan   Kenya

1 Listen and say. 1/10

2 Listen and read. 1/11

I'm from America.

I'm from Japan.

I'm from Kenya.

Jessica

Sumi

Adam

Justin

Nelson

I'm from England.

I'm from Poland.

10

1 Pupils learn and say the new words, paying special attention to their pronunciation. ⊃TB
2 Pupils listen to the two dialogues and read the sentences aloud. ⊃TB

3 Match and read.

1 Justin is from

2 Adam is from

3 Nelson is from

4 Jessica is from

5 Sumi is from

4 Listen and chant. 1/12 ♪

5 Write, match and colour.

Poland
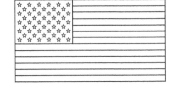

America

Japan

3 Pupils match the children with their home countries and read the sentences aloud.
4 Pupils listen to the chant and chant all together. ⊃TB
5 Pupils trace over the names of the countries, match them with the flags and colour the flags.

Wonderful world

This is a big family from Gabon.

1 Read and match.

1 Beata and Julia are twin sisters from France.

2 Akio and Fumito are cousins from Japan.

3 Billy and his family are from America.

2 Look and write.

1 Pupils read the sentences and match them with the correct picture.
2 Pupils complete a family tree. ⮌TB

The children are cousins.

Kazu and Ikki are twin brothers from Japan.

Class Project

My family

Prepare your family tree. Put pictures of your family members in the tree. You can write the family words below the pictures. Talk about the people in the poster in English.

DVD Club

photo album

photographs

smartphone

1 **Watch, tick and say.**

a photo album ☐ a kitchen ☐ a boy ☐
a living room ☐ a dog ☐ a bike ☐

2 **Watch, circle and say.**

Look at my family! This is my ...

1 **mummy / sister**   2 **daddy / grandpa**

3 **grandma / aunt**   4 **uncle / brother**

5 **sister / aunt**

3 **Watch and say.**

1 Pupils watch the DVD, tick the items they have seen and say the words.
2 Pupils watch the DVD again, circle the appropriate word and say the words.
3 Pupils watch the slideshows and repeat the words.

15

Review 1

1 Listen and stick.

1

Anna

2

Masu

3

Carmen

4

Kofi

5

Zadi

2 Read and match.

son   girl

uncle   granddaughter

grandson   aunt

daddy   grandma

grandpa   mummy

boy   daughter

3 Talk.

1 Pupils listen and stick the correct sticker under the photos and names of the speakers.
2 Pupils read the words and match them accordingly.
3 Pupils act out short dialogues. ⊃TB

I can! Family and friends

I already can!

1 I can listen, understand and point.

 ☐  ☐  ☐  ☐  ☐

2 I can say the names.

 ☐  ☐  ☐  ☐  ☐

3 I can:

☐ ask someone their name,

☐ tell someone my name

☐ ask someone about their age

☐ tell someone how old I am

☐ ask where someone is from

☐ tell someone where I am from

☐ talk about my family.

4 I can read.

☐ family ☐ boy ☐ son ☐ parents ☐ England

5 I can write.

boy   girl   big family   friend

My room

You will learn:
* to describe your room
* to talk about things you can do
* to ask about things others can do.

1 **Listen and say.** 1/15 💬

2 **Listen and chant.** 1/16 🎵

3 **Listen, chant and play.** 1/17 🎵 🎲

A new computer

bed   computer   armchair   old   new

1 Listen and say. 1/18

Story corner

2 Listen and read. 1/19

1 Pupils learn and say the new words, paying special attention to their pronunciation. ⟶TB
2 Pupils listen to the dialogue, follow the story and read the sentences. ⟶TB

3 Match, listen and say.

4 Play.

5 Write, circle and read.

1

armchair

2

bed

3

computer

4

chair

5

desk

3 Pupils match the objects with the characters, listen to the recording to check their answers, and repeat the sentences.
4 Pupils play *Sentence String.* ➲TB
5 Pupils trace over the words, circle the correct photos, and read the words aloud.

Maria's bedroom

  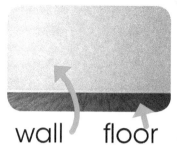

lamp   picture   carpet   wall   floor

1 **Listen and say.** 1/21

2 **Listen and read.** 1/22

This is Maria.
She's from Mexico.
This is her bedroom.
Maria likes her
bedroom.
There is a picture
on the wall. There is
a carpet on the floor.
The bed is big.
There are two lamps.
It is a nice bedroom.

1 Pupils learn and say the new words, paying special attention to their pronunciation. ⟳TB
2 Pupils listen to the recording, follow the text and read it aloud. ⟳TB

3 Listen and say. **1/23**

4 Stick, listen and say.  **1/24**

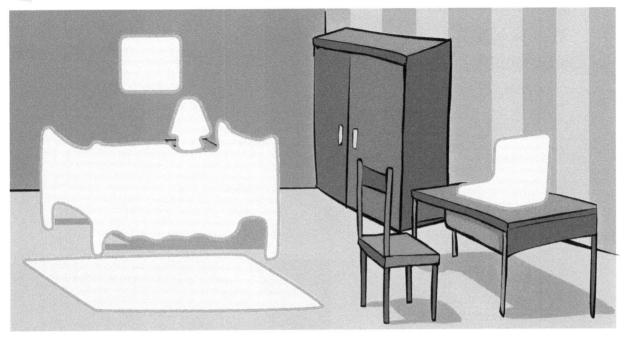

5 Write, match and read.

wall   lamp   floor

carpet   picture

3 Pupils listen to the questions and answer them.
4 Pupils stick the correct stickers, listen to the recording and repeat the phrases.
5 Pupils trace over the words, match them with the correct photos and read the words aloud.

23

I can dance.

play computer games

play chess

dance   draw

1 Listen and say. 1/25

2 Listen and read. 1/26

Can you play chess?

Yes, I can.

Can you draw a cat?

I can dance.

No, I can't.

3 Listen and sing. 1/27

1 Pupils learn and say the new words, paying special attention to their pronunciation. ➲TB
2 Pupils listen to the dialogues, point to the photos and read the sentences. ➲TB
3 Pupils listen to the song and sing all together. They do the actions. ➲TB

4 Listen, tick and say.

1

2

3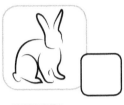

4

5 Write and read.

1 I can dance.   I can't dance.

2 I can jump.   I can't jump.

3 I can sing.   I can't sing.

4 I can swim.   I can't swim.

6 Play.

4 Pupils listen to the recording, tick ✓ the correct picture and repeat the sentences.
5 Pupils trace over the sentences that are true for them and read them aloud.
6 Pupils play *Memory*. ⟳TB

25

Wonderful world

There is a computer in this study.

Look at the flowers in the garden.

1 Play.

2 Look and write.

1 Pupils play *Where am I?* ➲TB
2 Pupils look at the clues, complete the crossword and find the hidden word.

The girl is in the garage.

This is a new attic.

Class Project

The room of my dreams

In pairs, make models of your rooms. Make furniture using boxes, pieces of paper and fabric. Describe your rooms in English.

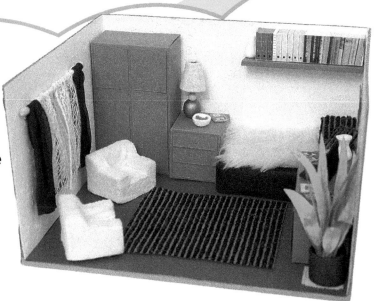

DVD club.

roof

window

hut

garden

1 Watch, number and say.

garden	☐	Jess's bedroom	☐
bathroom	☐	living room	☐
kitchen	☐	Tom's bedroom	☐

2 Watch, write and say.

J = Jess
T = Tom

1 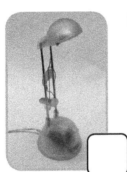 ☐

2  ☐

3  ☐

4  ☐

5  ☐

3 Watch and say.

1 Pupils watch the DVD, number the places in the correct order and say the words.
2 Pupils watch the DVD again and write 'J' for Jess or 'T' for Tom. Then they name the items.
3 Pupils watch the slideshows and repeat the words.

Review 2

1 Read, number and say.

1 old chair	6 new picture
2 old floor	7 new chair
3 old lamp	8 new floor
4 old computer	9 new lamp
5 old picture	10 new computer

2 Look and say.

3 Play.

1 Pupils read the phrases and number the photos accordingly. Then they name the items looking only at the photos.
2 Pupils say what Bob and Ann can do and can't do.
3 Pupils play *Find Your Pair*. ➲TB

 **My room**

I already can!

1 I can listen, understand and point.

2 I can say the names.

3 I can:

☐ describe my house and say the names of the rooms

☐ talk about what I can and can't do

☐ talk about what is new/old

☐ ask about things someone can or can't do.

☐ describe my room

4 I can read.

☐ draw ☐ dance ☐ old ☐ new ☐ play

5 I can write.

new house   old computer

Animals

You will learn:

- ✳ to describe animals
- ✳ to say the names of farm animals
- ✳ to describe the actions of animals in the pictures.

1 Listen and say.  🔊1/30 💬

2 Listen and chant. 🔊1/31 🎵

3 Talk. 💬

Lesson 1

My tail is short.

animals   short tail   long tail   fur   brown

1 Listen and say. 1/32 🔊

2 Listen and read. 1/33 🔊

1. Snap's got a long tail.

2. Bears have got short tails.

3. I haven't got a tail! I'm not a bear.

4. I haven't got a long tail but I've got nice brown fur.

1 Pupils learn and say the new words, paying special attention to their pronunciation. ➲TB
2 Pupils listen to the dialogue, follow the story and read the sentences. ➲TB

3 Listen and number.

4 Listen, sing and play.

5 Write, match and read.

1   long tail

2   short tail

3   brown fur

3 Pupils listen to the recording and number the photos in the correct order.
4 Pupils listen to the song, sing it and play all together. ➲TB
5 Pupils trace over the phrases, match them with the correct photos and read the phrases aloud..

35

Sheep

| sheep | lamb | grass | eat | white |

1 Listen and say. 1/36

2 Listen and read. 1/37

Look at the sheep. There is a mummy sheep and there are two lambs. A lamb is a baby sheep. The lambs have got white fur, short tails and long legs. Sheep eat grass. They are nice.

1 Pupils learn and say the new words, paying special attention to their pronunciation. ⊃TB
2 Pupils listen to the recording, follow the text and read it aloud. ⊃TB

3 **Write, tick and read.**

Sheep eat grass.

4 **Colour and say.**

5 **Listen, chant and play.**

3 Pupils trace over the sentence, tick the correct picture, and read the sentence aloud.
4 Pupils colour the picture according to the key and name the objects.
5 Pupils listen to the chant, chant it and play all together. ⟳TB

On the farm

farm   cow   duck   pig   horse

1 Listen and say. 1/39

2 Listen, number and read. 1/40

On the farm

The lambs are playing.

The horse is jumping.

The cow is eating grass.

The pigs are running.

The ducks are swimming.

1 Pupils learn and say the new words, paying special attention to their pronunciation. ⊃TB
2 Pupils listen to the dialogue, number the photos and read the sentences. ⊃TB

3 Look, stick and read.

1 **Look at the** _____ .

2 **The** _____ **is swimming.**

3 **The** _____ **are eating grass.**

4 **The** _____ **is jumping.**

5 **The** _____ **are playing with the ball.**

4 Write and read.

lamb   cow   pig   horse   duck

5 Listen, sing and play.

3 Pupils look at the picture, complete the sentences with the correct stickers and read the sentences aloud.
4 Pupils trace over the words and read them aloud.
5 Pupils listen to the song, sing it and play all together. ➲TB

Wonderful world

These goats are in a tree.

This donkey is very gentle.

1 Listen and sing. 1/42

2 Colour and say.

1 Pupils listen to the song and sing all together.
2 Pupils colour the pictures and name the animals.

This guinea pig is sweet.

These rabbits have got long ears.

Class Project

Fascinating animals

In pairs, make mini-books about a chosen group of animals. Illustrate the books and describe the animals in English.

DOGS

YORKSHIRE TERRIER

It's small.
It's got long fur.
It's got small ears.

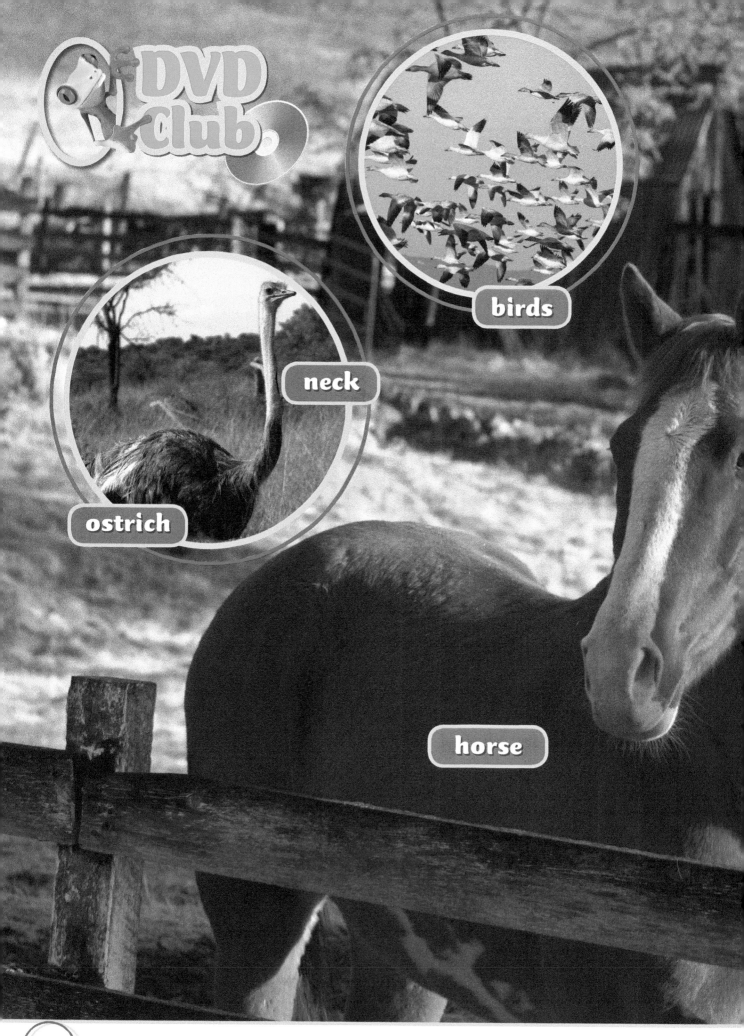

DVD
club.

birds

neck

ostrich

horse

1 Watch, colour and say.

2 Watch, circle and read.

1 The horse is   running   eating .

2 The cow is   eating   running .

3 The lambs are   jumping   swimming .

3 Watch and say.

1 Pupils watch the DVD, colour the animals they have seen in the DVD and name them.
2 Pupils watch the DVD again, circle the correct words and read the sentences aloud.
3 Pupils watch the slideshows and repeat the words.

Review 3

1 Listen and number.

2 Look and read.

This is a . It is very big. It is

and . It has got long  and

a long . It likes  and .

3 Play.

1 Pupils listen to the recording and number the photos in the correct order.
2 Pupils look at the text with pictures and read it. ➲TB
3 Pupils play *Call Out*. ➲TB

I can! **Animals**

I already can!

1 I can listen, understand and point. 1/44

 ☐  ☐  ☐  ☐  ☐

2 I can say the names.

 ☐  ☐  ☐  ☐  ☐

3 I can:

☐ talk about the animal I've got or I haven't got at home

☐ describe the animal

☐ name the farm animals

☐ describe the actions of animals in the pictures.

4 I can read.

☐ cow ☐ short ☐ long ☐ eat ☐ animals

5 I can write.

lamb   brown   short tail

Unit 4

Places

You will learn:
* to advise someone how to cross the street
* to suggest doing something together
* to say the names of places in the town.

1 **Listen and say.** (1/45)

2 **Listen and chant.** (1/46)

3 **Listen and draw.** (1/47)

Stop!

 go stop

 cross

 left

 right

 Be careful!

1 Listen and say.

Story corner

2 Listen and read.

48

1 Pupils learn and say the new words, paying special attention to their pronunciation. ⟳TB
2 Pupils listen to the dialogue, follow the story and read the sentences. ⟳TB

3 Listen and chant. 🎵

4 Look, stick and read. 👀 💬 🔍

Don't [   ] !   [   ] !

Be [   ] !   Look [   ] !

Go [   ] !   [   ] go!

5 Play.

3 Pupils listen to the chant and chant all together. They do the actions. ➲TB
4 Pupils look at the pictures, stick the correct stickers and read the phrases.
5 Pupils play *Red Light, Green Light*. ➲TB

49

Market on water

market   water   food   buy   shop

1 Listen and say. 1/51

2 Listen and read. 1/52

Look at this market. It's in Thailand.
It's on water. The boats are shops.
You can buy food at this market.
Are there any markets on water in
your country?

1 Pupils learn and say the new words, paying special attention to their pronunciation. ⊃TB
2 Pupils listen to the recording, follow the text and read it aloud. ⊃TB

3 Listen and number.

4 Write and read.

market on water

buy food   toy shop

5 Play.

3 Pupils listen to the dialogues and number the pictures in the correct order.
4 Pupils trace over the phrases and read them aloud.
5 Pupils play *Hunt the Thimble.* ➾TB

51

London

museum   church   park   street   bridge   lots of

1 **Listen and say.**

2 **Listen and read.**

It's a church. It's big and old.

Are there any museums in London?

Yes, there are.

There are lots of bridges in London.

There are lots of parks in London.

There are lots of shops on this street but there aren't any markets on water.

1 Pupils learn and say the new words, paying special attention to their pronunciation. ➲TB
2 Pupils listen to the dialogue, point to the photos and and read the sentences. ➲TB

3 **Listen and match.**

1    

2    

3    

4   

5    

4 **Listen and sing.**

5 **Write and read.**

British Museum   Hyde Park

Oxford Street   Tower Bridge

3 Pupils listen to the dialogues and match the characters with the places.
4 Pupils listen to the song and sing all together.
5 Pupils trace over the phrases and read them aloud.

Wonderful world

This is a cinema in Paris, France.

This is a church in Barcelona, Spain.

1 Make and say.

2 Circle and read.

churchparkcinemamuseummarketshop

1 Pupils make a jigsaw and say what's in the picture. ➲TB
2 Pupils circle the words and read them aloud. ➲TB

This is a big theatre in Sydney, Australia.

This is a museum in Bilbao, Spain.

Class Project

A map of your neigbourhood
In groups, make a map of your neighbourhood. Draw important places on the map. Talk about the places on the map in English.

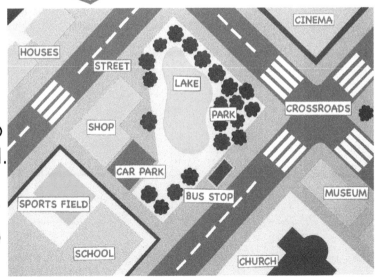

HOUSES
CINEMA
STREET
LAKE
SHOP
PARK
CROSSROADS
CAR PARK
BUS STOP
SPORTS FIELD
MUSEUM
SCHOOL
CHURCH

Pupils do a class project. ⮑TB

DVD Club

cooking pot

camera

take photos

Thailand

people

hat

1 Watch, number and say.

2 Watch, circle and say.

At the market on water, in Thailand, you can see …

a cooking pot

cameras

books

bananas

oranges

flowers   boats

hats   food

3 Watch and say.

1 Pupils watch the DVD, number the photos in the correct order and say the words.
2 Pupils watch the DVD again, circle the words they have heard and say them.
3 Pupils watch the slideshows and repeat the words.

Review 4

1 Write, circle and read.

1 old church

2 long street

3 small shop

2 Listen and number.

3 Play.

1 Pupils trace over the phrases, circle the correct pictures and read the phrases.
2 Pupils listen to the recording and number the pictures in the correct order.
3 Pupils play *Treasure Maps.* ➡TB

 **Places**

I already can!

1 I can listen, understand and point.

2 I can say the names.

3 I can:

☐ advise someone how to cross the street

☐ say the names of places in the town

☐ suggest doing something together

☐ give information about London.

4 I can read.

☐ shop ☐ street ☐ market ☐ right ☐ go

5 I can write.

garden   stop   Be careful!

Pupils do the self-evaluation.

59

Clothes

You will learn:
* to say what you are wearing
* to ask about quantity
* to say what you are doing at that time
* to count to fifteen.

1 **Listen and say.** 2/1

2 **Listen and chant.** 2/2

3 **Listen and colour.** 2/3

A jacket for Chatty

jacket   shoes   clothes   eleven   twelve

1 Listen and say. 2/4

Story corner

2 Listen and read. 2/5

1

Happy birthday, Chatty!

Thanks!

2

How many jackets have you got, Chatty?

Eleven.

3

How many friends are there?

Chatty isn't here. Where is she?

4

Now there are twelve friends.

Let's dance!

1 Pupils learn and say the new words, paying special attention to their pronunciation. ➲TB
2 Pupils listen to the dialogue, follow the story and read the sentences. ➲TB

3 Listen, write and circle. (2/6)

1

2

3

4

5

4 Listen, stick and sing. (2/7)

5 Play.

3 Pupils listen to the dialogues, write the numbers in the boxes and circle the correct pictures.
4 Pupils listen to the song, stick the correct stickers and sing the song all together.
5 Pupils play *Chinese Whispers.* ⟳TB

63

A school in Africa

 study    teacher    wear    uniform    shirt

1 Listen and say. 2/8

2 Listen and read.   2/9

This is a small school in Africa. The children are studying.
There is a teacher, too.
The children are wearing uniforms: green and white shirts
and green sweaters. The teacher is wearing nice clothes.

1 Pupils learn and say the new words, paying special attention to their pronunciation. ➲TB
2 Pupils listen to the recording, follow the text and read it aloud. ➲TB

3 Read and circle.

1 The girl is wearing a uniform.

2 The teacher is eating.

3 The boy is studying.

4 Listen and chant.

5 Write and read.

I'm wearing

3 Pupils read the sentences and circle the correct pictures.
4 Pupils listen to the chant and chant all together. They do the actions. ⊃TB
5 Pupils trace over the words and complete the sentence. They read their sentence aloud.

65

My sister's shoes

sandals   dress   socks   thirteen   fourteen   fifteen

1 Listen and say. 2/11

2 Listen and read. 2/12

1 Pupils learn and say the new words, paying special attention to their pronunciation. ➲TB
2 Pupils listen to the dialogue, point to the photo and read the sentences. ➲TB

3 Listen, match and chant. 2/13

13

14

15

4 Look and say.

5 Draw and talk.

3 Pupils listen to the chant, match the numbers to the pictures and chant all together.
4 Pupils look at the picture and say what Mum, Dad, Grandpa and the daughter are wearing.
5 Pupils draw themselves, ask and answer questions in pairs and draw their friends. ➲TB

Wonderful world

Look at the boys from Thailand.
They are wearing masks.

Welcome to Poland.
The children are wearing folk costumes.

1 Match and say.

2 Draw and talk.

1 Pupils match the children with the objects, say where the children are from and name the objects.
2 Pupils design an imaginary folk costume and talk about it. ⊃TB

This girl is from Japan.
She is wearing a kimono.

Let's go to Scotland.
The boy is wearing a kilt.

Class Project

Fashion show
Organise a class fashion show. Bring clothes from home. Make a film. Describe the models in English.

DVD Club.

wash

river

washing machine

1 Watch, tick and say.

 ☐

 ☐

 ☐

 ☐

 ☐

 ☐

 ☐

 ☐

2 Watch, match and say.

a T-shirt

a jacket

socks

shorts

a dress

sandals

shoes

3 Watch and say.

1 Pupils watch the DVD, tick the clothes Jess is wearing and name them.
2 Pupils watch the DVD again, match the words to Tom or Jess and say the words.
3 Pupils watch the slideshows and repeat the words.

Review 5

1 Listen and number. 2/14

2 Write and read.

jacket market shoes food dress shirt
church duck sandals carpet socks

clothes: _____

_____

3 Play.

1 Pupils listen to the recording and number the pictures in the correct order.
2 Pupils decide which words are items of clothing, write them in the space provided and read them aloud.
3 Pupils play the *Guessing Game.* ➲TB

I can! **Clothes**

I already can!

1 I can listen, understand and point. 2/15

□   □   □   □   □

2 I can say the numbers.

13 12 15 11 14

□   □   □   □   □

3 I can:

□ say what I am wearing   □ ask about quantity

□ say what I am doing at   □ count to fifteen.
  that time

4 I can read.

□ study   □ sandals   □ uniform   □ I'm wearing socks.

5 I can write.

socks and shoes nice teacher

Pupils do the self-evaluation.

Free time

You will learn:
* to talk about your free time
* to ask about everyday routines and talk about them
* to count to twenty.

1 Listen and say. 2/16

2 Listen and chant. 2/17

3 Play.

75

I watch TV.

 ride a bike  watch TV listen to music

16 sixteen **17** seventeen

 every day   at the weekend

1 **Listen and say.** 2/18

2 **Listen and read.** 2/19

Story corner

1
I ride my bike every day.

2
I watch TV at the weekend.

3
Do you like music, Honey?
Yes, I do.

4
This is song seventeen.

1 Pupils learn and say the new words, paying special attention to their pronunciation. ⊃TB
2 Pupils listen to the dialogue, follow the story and read the sentences. ⊃TB

3 Listen and tick. 2/20

	John	Anna
bicycle	☐ yes, every day ☐ yes, at the weekend ☐ no	☐ yes, every day ☐ yes, at the weekend ☐ no
radio	☐ yes, every day ☐ yes, at the weekend ☐ no	☐ yes, every day ☐ yes, at the weekend ☐ no
TV	☐ yes, every day ☐ yes, at the weekend ☐ no	☐ yes, every day ☐ yes, at the weekend ☐ no

4 Listen and chant. 2/21

5 Write and read.

ride a bike   watch TV

listen to music

3 Pupils listen to the dialogues and tick the correct boxes.
4 Pupils listen to the chant and chant all together. They do the actions. ⟳TB
5 Pupils trace over the phrases and read them aloud.

I ride a skateboard.

skateboard   slow   fast   win   race

1 Listen and say. `2/22`

2 Listen and read. `2/23`

Hello. I'm George and this is my brother Tim.
We've got skateboards. I ride my skateboard every day.
I win races because my skateboard is fast.
Tim's skateboard is slow but he's happy.

1 Pupils learn and say the new words, paying special attention to their pronunciation. ➲TB
2 Pupils listen to the recording, follow the text and read it aloud. ➲TB

3 Listen, write and read.

| fast   slow   fast |

1 Grandpa's bike is _____

2 My skateboard is _____

3 Dad's car is _____

4 Listen and chant.

5 Make and read. ✂ 💬

bike   I   my

ride   at the weekend.

I ride my bike at the weekend.

3 Pupils listen to the recording and complete the sentences with the correct words from the box. Then they
  trace over the sentences, colour in the pictures and read the sentences aloud.
4 Pupils listen to the chant and chant all together. ➲TB
5 Pupils cut out the words and make sentences. They stick them in their notebooks and read them aloud. ➲TB

79

Sandra's weekend

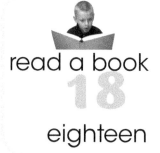 read a book
18
eighteen

 phone a friend
19
nineteen

 do homework
20
twenty

1 Listen and say. 2/26

2 Listen and read. 2/27

What do you do at the weekend?

Do you watch TV?

At the weekend, I do my homework with Mummy.

No, I don't. I play computer games.

I phone my friends.

Do you read books at the weekend?

Yes, I do. I read books with my brother.

1 Pupils learn and say the new words, paying special attention to their pronunciation. ⟳TB
2 Pupils listen to the dialogue, point to the photos and read the sentences. ⟳TB

3 Look and read. 👀 💬

My name is Harry. At the weekend I in the living room and in my bedroom. Song **20** is my favourite song. I . I've got **18** friends. I  in my bedroom . Then I  . There are **19** books in my bedroom.

4 Listen and chant. 🎧 2/28 🎵

1	2	3	4	5
6	7	8	9	10
11	12	13	14	15
16	17	18	19	20

5 Look, circle and read. 👀 ✏️ 💬

1 read   2 phone

3 watch   4 win

3 Pupils look at the text with pictures and read it.
4 Pupils listen to the chant and chant all together. ➲TB
5 Pupils circle the correct picture and read the phrases aloud.

81

Wonderful world

Hopscotch is fun.
I like hopping.

I like **Noughts and Crosses**.
I often win.

1 Play and say.

2 Circle and read.

winplayweekendoftenhoppingrace

1 Pupils play *Rock, Scissors, Paper* and say the words.
2 Pupils circle the words and read them aloud.

Can you play Rock, Scissors, Paper?

We play Hide and Seek at the weekend.

Class Project

Your hobby
In English, talk about your hobbies and what you like to do in your free time. If possible, show your collections to the class.

Pupils do the class project. ➲TB

DVD Club

China

pavement

learn to ride

1 Watch, tick and say.

 In my free time, I …

	Yes	No
ride a bike		
watch TV		
listen to music		
read books		
ride a skateboard		
win races		

town

2 Watch, circle and say.

a town   two girls   two boys
skateboards   bikes   cars
flowers   trees   huts   pavement

3 Watch and say.

1 Pupils watch the DVD, tick the correct boxes and say the sentences.
2 Pupils watch the DVD again, circle the items they have seen and say the words.
3 Pupils watch the slideshows and repeat the words.

Review 6

1 Listen and stick. 2/29

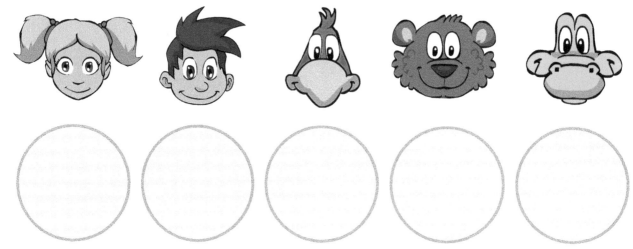

2 Write and read.

> homework   skateboard   race

1 ride a

2 do my

3 win a

3 Listen and sing. 2/30 ♪

1 Pupils listen to the recording and stick the correct stickers.
2 Pupils trace over the phrases, complete them using the correct word from the box and read them aloud.
3 Pupils listen to the song and sing it all together.

I can! Free time

I already can! 🙂 😐 🙁

1 I can listen, understand and point.

     😮

2 I can say the numbers.

19 17 16 20 18

⬜ ⬜ ⬜ ⬜ ⬜ 😮

3 I can:

⬜ say what I do in my free time

⬜ ask about everyday routines and talk about them

⬜ count to twenty. 😮

4 I can read.

⬜ read a book ⬜ fast skateboard ⬜ listen to music 😮

5 I can write.

<u>at the weekend</u>   <u>I win races.</u> 😮

Unit 7 Sports

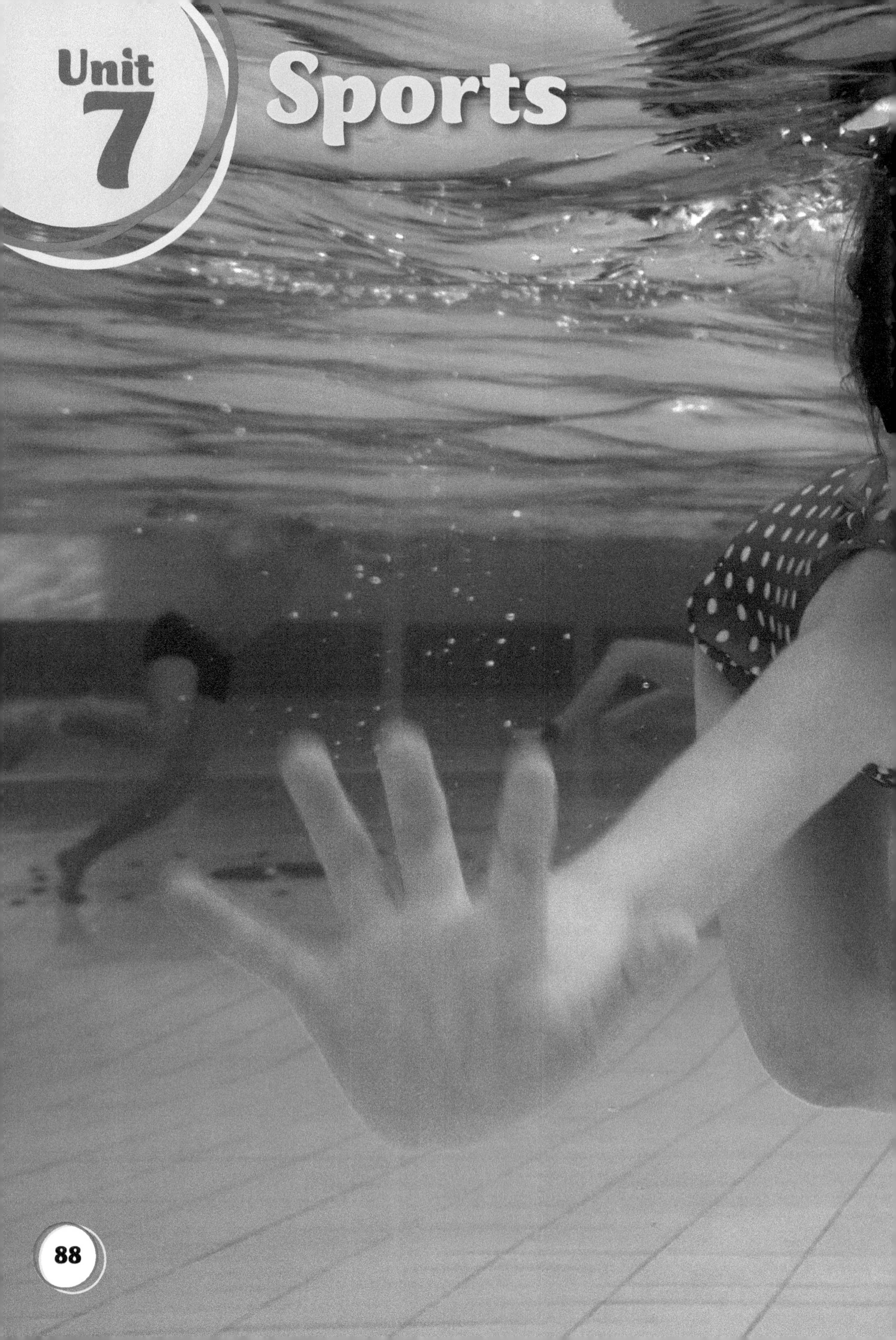

You will learn:
* to talk about your favourite sport
* to ask others about their favourite sport
* to talk about winter sports.

1 **Listen and say.** 2/32

2 **Listen and chant.** 2/33 ♫

3 **Look and number.**

Do you like sport?

basketball football volleyball tennis swimming

1 Listen and say. 2/34

2 Listen and read. 2/35

Story corner

1
I like swimming.

I don't like swimming.

2
I like football.

I don't like football.

3
I like basketball and Kate likes volleyball.

4
I don't like sport but I love my tennis computer game.

1 Pupils learn and repeat the new words, paying special attention to their pronunciation. ➲TB
2 Pupils listen to the dialogue, follow the story and read the sentences. ➲TB

3 Play.

4 Listen and stick. 2/36

1

2

3

4

5

6

5 Write and read.

swimming basketball volleyball football tennis

I like

I don't like

3 Pupils play the *Guessing Game.* ➲TB
4 Pupils listen to the recording and stick a happy face or a sad face sticker.
5 Pupils trace over the phrases, complete them with words from the box and read them aloud.

91

Football

kick   fall   score a goal   match   radio   sometimes

1 Listen and say.

2 Listen and read.

This is Pedro. He is from Brazil. Pedro plays football every day. He runs and sometimes he falls. He kicks the ball and scores goals. Pedro hasn't got a TV. He listens to football matches on the radio.

1 Pupils learn and repeat the new words, paying special attention to their pronunciation. ⮑TB
2 Pupils listen to the recording, follow the text and read it aloud. ⮑TB

3 Read and match.

1    score a goal

2    kick

3    listen to the radio

4    fall

4 Listen and sing. 2/39

5 Read and talk.

Do you play football?

Yes, I do.

No, I don't.

score a goal   ride a bike   fall
listen to the radio   watch matches

3 Pupils read the phrases and match them with the pictures.
4 Pupils listen to the song and sing all together. They do the actions. ⊃TB
5 In groups, pupils ask and answer questions using phrases from the box. ⊃TB

93

Winter sports

winter   ride a sledge   ice hockey   skiing   ice skating

1 Listen and say. 2/40

2 Listen and read. 2/41

I like winter because skiing is my favourite sport.

Pam loves ice skating.

I ride a sledge with my friends at the weekend.

My brother Robert plays ice hockey at school.

1 Pupils learn and say the new words, paying special attention to their pronunciation. ⏎TB
2 Pupils listen to the dialogue, point to the photos and read the sentences. ⏎TB

3 Listen and sing. 2/42 ♩

4 Look and stick. 👀

Sports

5 Write and read.

> ice skating   ice hockey   skiing

1

Robert plays

2

Amy likes

3

Pam loves

3 Pupils listen to the song and sing it all together.
4 Pupils look at the picture and stick the stickers in the correct places.
5 Pupils trace over the phrases, complete them with words from the box and read them aloud.

95

Wonderful world

Show jumping is fun to watch.

1 Match and read.

show jumping

karate

ice hockey

tennis

Water-skiing is fun. It's a great sport.

2 Make and say.

1 Pupils match the photos with the words and read the words aloud.
2 Pupils make a mobile and name the sports. ⊃TB

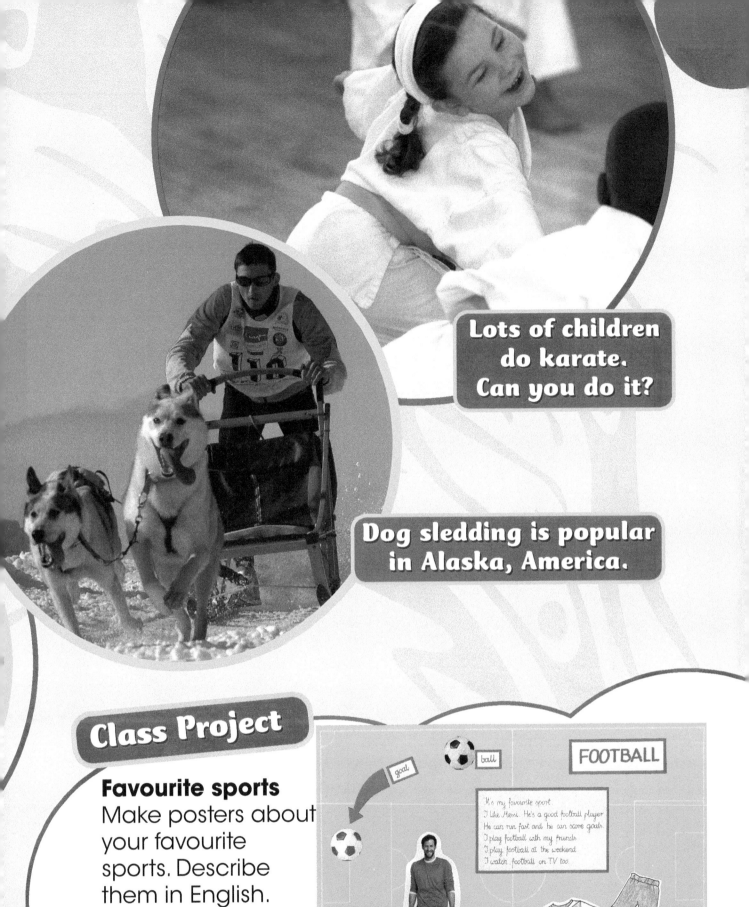

Lots of children do karate. Can you do it?

Dog sledding is popular in Alaska, America.

Class Project

Favourite sports
Make posters about your favourite sports. Describe them in English. Which sport is the most popular in your class?

FOOTBALL

goal

ball

It's my favourite sport.
I like Messi. He's a good football player.
He can run fast and he can score goals.
I play football with my friends.
I play football at the weekend.
I watch football on TV too.

footballer

socks

T-shirt

shorts

shoes

player

goalkeeper

net

1 Watch, colour and say.

2 Watch, circle and say.

1   I like   tennis   swimming .

2   I don't like   tennis   football .

3   I like   skiing   ice hockey .

4   I don't like   ice skating   skiing .

5   I like   volleyball   basketball .

6   We like   volleyball   football .

3 Watch and say.

1 Pupils watch the DVD, colour the correct pictures and name the sports.
2 Pupils watch the DVD again, circle the correct words and say the words.
3 Pupils watch the slideshows and repeat the words.

Review **7**

1 Read and circle.

1 ride	a book	a sledge	a ball
2 watch	TV	homework	winter
3 play	ice hockey	skiing	ice skating
4 win	swimming	a goal	a race
5 listen to	music	ice hockey	a race
6 score	a goal	a book	homework
7 kick	a race	a ball	a radio

2 Listen and number.

3 Play.

1 Pupils read the words and circle the correct ending for each phrase.
2 Pupils listen to the recording and number the pictures in the correct order.
3 Pupils play *What's Missing?* ⊃TB

 **Sports**

I already can! 😊 😐 ☹️

1 I can listen, understand and point. 2/44

 ☐  ☐  ☐  ☐  ☐

2 I can say the names. 👀 💬

 ☐  ☐  ☐  ☐  ☐

3 I can:

☐ talk about my favourite sport   ☐ ask others about their favourite sport

☐ talk about how to play football   ☐ talk about winter sports.

4 I can read.

☐ score a goal   ☐ win a match   ☐ Harry plays ice hockey.   ☐ winter sports

5 I can write.

I love football. I kick the ball.

This is me!

You will learn:
* to ask how others feel
* to say how you feel
* to talk about your birthday party.

1 Listen and say. 2/45

2 Look and say.

3 Play.

103

Goodbye!

ill   bag   smile   fly   cry   better

1 Listen and say. (2/46)

2 Listen and read. (2/47)

Story corner

1

Are you ill?

I'm hot.

2

How are you?

I'm better.

3

How are you, Chatty?

I'm OK now!

4

We're all happy.

1 Pupils learn and repeat the new words, paying special attention to their pronunciation. ⟳TB
2 Pupils listen to the dialogue, follow the story and read the sentences. ⟳TB

3 Circle, colour and say.

crayon

ball

water

banana

lamp

flowers

shirt

bag

teddy bear

4 Listen and chant. 🔊 2/48 🎵

5 Look, stick and read. 👀 💬 💭

Oh, my leg!

!

Are you [ ] ?

Yes, I am. I can't [ ] .

Don't [ ] .

3 Pupils circle the names of things Chatty has got, colour the picture and describe it.
4 Pupils listen to the chant and chant all together. They do the actions. ⊃TB
5 Pupils look at the pictures, stick the correct stickers and read the phrases aloud.

105

Favourite pastimes

roller skating   helmet   people   summer   often

1 Listen and say. 2/49

2 Listen and read. 2/50

The girls are from America. They are in a roller skating race. Two girls are wearing helmets. Lots of people are watching the race. People often go roller skating in summer and ice skating in winter.

1 Pupils learn and say the new words, paying special attention to their pronunciation. ⟳TB
2 Pupils listen to the recording, follow the text and read it aloud. ⟳TB

3 Listen and number.

4 Listen and chant.

5 Write and read.

skiing   playing ice hockey   roller skating   riding a skateboard
ice skating   riding a bike   riding a sledge   swimming

It's summer. I'm

It's winter. I'm

3 Pupils listen to the recording and number the pictures accordingly.
4 Pupils listen to the chant and chant all together. They do the actions. ⊃TB
5 Pupils trace over the sentences, complete them with words from the box and read them aloud.

107

party hat   drink   juice   balloon   candle

1 Listen and say. 2/53

2 Listen and read. 2/54

I've got lots of presents and balloons today.

Look! I've got a party hat.

My dog is wearing a party hat, too!

Let's eat some cake and drink some juice now!

1 Pupils learn and say the new words, paying special attention to their pronunciation. ↪TB
2 Pupils listen to the dialogue, point to the photos and read the sentences. ↪TB

3 Stick and say.

4 Play.

5 Look, write and read.

1 I've got a  _____

2 I've got two  _____

3 There are eight  _____ on the cake.

4 I drink lots of _____ in summer.

3 Pupils stick the correct stickers on the picture and name the objects.
4 Pupils play *Chinese Whispers.* ⊃TB
5 Pupils look at the pictures, write the words and read the sentences aloud.

109

Wonderful world

I like flowers. Sunflowers are my favourite flowers.

Look at me! I like riding my bike with my grandpa.

Bob is from England.

Muna is from South Africa.

1 Read and write.

Name	Place	Likes
Indira	_____	playing computer games
_____	England	riding a bike
Muna	_____	_____
_____	China	_____

2 Listen and sing. 2/55 ♪

1 Pupils read the text and complete the table. ⊃TB
2 Pupils listen to the song and sing it all together.

Ching is from China.

I like reading books.
This book is about pets.

I like playing computer games.
This is my mum's computer.

Indira is from India.

Class Project

Mini time-capsule

Write a few sentences about yourself. Put them into a capsule to be opened in a few years' time. Think about how different your life will be then!

I'm Steve. I'm eight.
I like sport and books.
I ride a skateboard and I swim at the weekend.
I read books every day.
I've got a sister, Anna.
She's ten. She likes winter but I like summer.
I like animals and I've got a cat, Blackie. It's big and black.
I've got lots of friends.

DVD Club

knee pads

sunglasses

roller skates

1 Watch, tick and say.

 ☐

 ☐

 ☐

 ☐

 ☐

 ☐

 ☐

 ☐

2 Watch, circle and say.

1   is ill.

2  is wearing a helmet.

3  is drinking juice.

4  has got a balloon for Tom.

5  has got lots of balloons for Tom.

3 Watch and say.

1 Pupils watch the DVD, tick the correct photos and name the objects.
2 Pupils watch the DVD again, circle the correct photos and read the sentences aloud.
3 Pupils watch the slideshows and repeat the words.

Review 8

1 Write, match and say.

candle   present   helmet

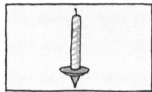      

party hat   balloon   bag

2 Listen and circle. 2/56

1 **Snap is**	ill	OK .
2 **Billy's favourite sport is**	ice skating	roller skating .
3 **Tom has got eight**	balloons	candles .
4 **Vicky likes**	winter	summer .

3 Read and draw.

How are you?

 I'm OK.

I'm crying.

I'm ill.

I'm great.

 114

1 Pupils trace over the words, match them to the pictures and read them aloud.
2 Pupils listen to the recording and circle the correct ending for each sentence.
3 Pupils read the phrases and draw happy or sad faces.

 **This is me!**

I already can! 😊 😐 ☹

1 I can listen, understand and point.

 ☐  ☐  ☐  ☐  ☐

2 I can say the names.

 ☐  ☐  ☐  ☐  ☐

3 I can:

☐ ask someone how she/he feels

☐ say how I feel

☐ talk about my birthday party.

4 I can read.

☐ party hat   ☐ I'm ill.   ☐ How are you?   ☐ Goodbye!

5 I can write.

She's flying. _____   I'm better. _____

Celebrations   New Year

fireworks

sparkler

midnight

streamers

1 Listen and say. (2/58)

2 Listen and read. (2/59)

We've got sparklers.

Look at the fireworks. It's midnight.

I've got streamers.

3 Make and say.

4 Listen and sing. (2/60)

1 Pupils learn and say the new words, paying special attention to their pronunciation. ⊃TB
2 Pupils listen to the dialogue, point to the photos and read the sentences.
3 Pupils make a jigsaw and name the objects. ⊃TB
4 Pupils listen to the song and sing it all together.

Mother's Day

 bunch of flowers

 box of chocolates

 kiss

 hug

1 **Listen and say.**

2 **Listen and read.**

A box of chocolates and a big hug for you.

I've got a bunch of flowers for you.

3 **Listen and sing.**

4 **Make and write.**

1 Pupils learn and say the new words, paying special attention to their pronunciation. ⏎TB
2 Pupils listen to the dialogues, point to the photos and read the sentences.
3 Pupils listen to the song and sing it all together.
4 Pupils make Mother's Day cards and write the greetings inside. ⏎TB

117

The Hare and the Tortoise

hare   tortoise   bird   fox   mouse

1 Listen and say. 2/64

2 Listen and read. 2/65

1 Hello.

Look! It's our friend, the tortoise.

2 I'm fast and you're slow!

You're riding a bike.

3 I can run. Can you run?

No, I can't, but I can win a race.

4 I'm fast and you're slow!

I'm slow but I don't stop.

1 Pupils learn and say the new words, paying special attention to their pronunciation. ⊃TB
2 Pupils listen to the dialogue, follow the story and read the sentences. ⊃TB

walk   sleep   laugh   winner

3 Play.

NATIONAL GEOGRAPHIC
L E A R N I N G

Hopscotch Pupil's Book 2

Jennifer Heath

Publisher: Gavin McLean

Editorial Manager: Claire Merchant

Project Manager: Dorothy Robertson

Editor: Carole Hughes

Head of Production: Celia Jones

Art Director cover: Alex von Dallwitz

Senior Designer cover: Cari Wynkoop

Compositor: MPS Limited

Audio Producer: Liz Hammond

Acknowledgements:

Audio recorded at Motivation Sound Studios and GFS-PRO Studio.

Music composed by Evdoxia Banani and Vagelis Markontonis

Production at GFS-PRO Studio by George Flamouridis

For permission to use material from this text or product, submit all requests online at **cengage.com/permissions**

Further permissions questions can be emailed to **permissionrequest@cengage.com.**

ISBN: 978-1-4080-9798-4

National Geographic Learning
Cheriton House, North Way, Andover, Hampshire, SP10 5BE
United Kingdom

Cengage Learning is a leading provider of customised learning solutions with office locations around the globe, including Singapore, the United Kingdom, Australia, Mexico, Brazil and Japan. Locate our local office at **international.cengage.com/region**

Cengage Learning products are represented in Canada by Nelson Education Ltd.

Visit National Geographic Learning online at **ngl.cengage.com**
Visit our corporate website at **www.cengage.com**

Cover Photo Cesare Naldi/Getty Images

Shutterstock:
pp 1 tr, b, 2, 3, 6 tml, tm, tmr, tr, 7, 8, 9, 10, 11, 13 mr, 14, 15 mr, 16, 17 a-h, i-k, 20, 21, 22 tl, tml, tmr, tr, 23, 24 tl, tml, tmr, tr, br, 25, 26, 28, 29 b, 30, 31, 32-33, 34, 35, 36, 37, 38, 40, 41, 42, 44, 45, 48, 49, 50, 52, 53, 54, 55 tr, 56, 57 tl, tm, tr, ml, mr, m, 58, 59, 62, 64, 66, 68, 69 b-f, 70, 71 a, c, e, g, 72, 73, 74-75, 76, 77, 78, 80, 81, 82, 83, 84, 86, 87, 88-89, 90, 91, 92 a-e, 94, 96, 97, 98, 99 a, b, c, d, e, f, 100, 101, 104, 106, 108, 110 t, 111, 112, 113 a, d, 113 f, g, 114, 115, 116, 117

National Geographic:
pp 1 tl (Bruce Dale/National Geographic Creative), 4-5 (David Evans/National Geographic Creative), 12 (Lynn Johnson/National Geographic Creative), 13 tl (James A. Sugar/National Geographic Creative), 18-19 (Tim Laman/National Geographic Creative), 22 b (Raul Tauzon/National Geographic Creative), 27 tr (Greg Dale/National Geographic Creative), 42 bkgd (Rich Reid/National Geographic Creative), 46-47 (Michael Melford/National Geographic Creative), 60 (Michael & Jennifer Lewis/National Geographic Creative), 92 f (Cristina Mittermeier/National Geographic/Getty Images), 102-103 (Amy Toensing/National Geographic Creative)

Others:
6 tl (Image Source/Alamy), 15 ml (Zooid Pictures), 17 f (Yuri/E+/Getty Images), 17 g (Image Source/Alamy), 24 ml (Yuri/E+/Getty Images), 24 bl (KidStock/Blend Images/Corbis), 27 ml (Andreas Vitting/imageBROKER/Corbis), 29 m (68/Gk Hart/Vikki Hart/Ocean/Corbis), 29 ml, mr, bl, br (Zooid Pictures), 55 ml (Xavier Vila/Getty Images), 57 b (Zooid Pictures), 64 (Dbimages/Stock Photo/Alamy), 69 a (Micha Klootwijk/Stock Photo/Alamy), 71 b, d, f, h-j (Zooid Pictures), 85 (Zooid Pictures), 99 h-m (Zooid Pictures), 110 mr (Comstock/Getty Images), 113 b, c, e, h-m (Zooid Pictures)

Printed in the United Kingdom by Ashford Colour Press Ltd
Print Number 02   Print Year 2022

MIX
Paper from responsible sources
FSC® C011748

Unit 1, page 16

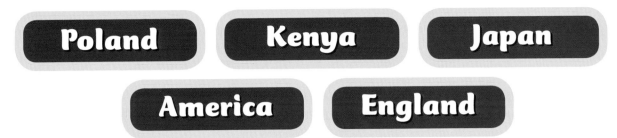

Poland Kenya Japan

America England

Unit 2, page 23

Unit 3, page 39

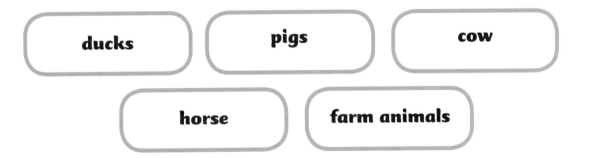

ducks pigs cow

horse farm animals

Unit 4, page 49

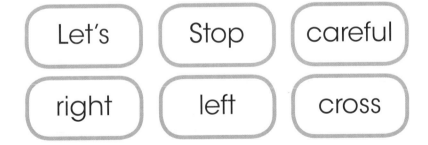

Let's Stop careful

right left cross

Unit 5, page 63

Unit 6, page 86

Unit 7, page 91

Unit 7, page 95

ice hockey	sledge	snow
ice skating	Winter	skiing

Unit 8, page 105

ill	cry	Smile	fly

Unit 8, page 109

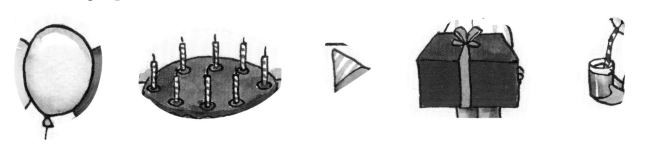